Spirit of Hula

MANA O HULA

Essence of Hula
Warren Rapozo Artist Paris, France

Spirit of Hula

MANA O HULA

Leilani Petranek

Mutual Publishing

A portion of the proceeds from royalties of *Spirit of Hula* will benefit
Halau Kaleihulumamo, 'Iolani Luahine's dream of a halau and resource
center for adults and children.

Endpaper artwork: *Beautiful Wahine* by C.H. Davis
Cover artwork: *Essence of Hula* byWarren Rapozo

ISBN 1-56647-693-3

Library of Congress Catalog Card Number: 2004112035

Design by Wanni

First Printing, October 2004
1 2 3 4 5 6 7 8 9

Mutual Publishing, LLC
1215 Center Street, Suite 210
Honolulu, Hawai'i 96816
Ph: 808-732-1709 / Fax: 808-734-4094
email: mutual@mutualpublishing.com
www.mutualpublishing.com

Printed in Korea

Aia Lā o Pele
Sylef Artist Paris, France

#

FLORENCE GRACE KINI, JOHN KA'APUNI KINI
& ETIENNE AURELIUS TRILLO

Hula Dancer Leilani
Florence Grace Kini Kaua'i, Hawai'i

E ʻio e

O ʻio, o stand, o bird

E ʻio e, eʻio e, e ku, e manu e

combine prayers to overcome, hakalau,

ke alu aku nei ka pule, ia hakalau,

The gods dwell in the woodlands

Noho ana ke akua i ka nahelehele

Hidden away in the mist in the low-hanging rainbow

I alai ʻia e ke kīʻohuʻohu e ka ua koko

Being sheltered by the heavens clear

ʻO nā kino malu i ka lani   Malu e hoe

our path of any disturbance—

E hōʻolu mai ana o ke akua i kona

we call to the gods to inspire us

kahu o mākou

Inspire and dwell with us and give us freedom

ʻo mākou noa e...

Poni Kamauʻu

viii

RIBUTE

ʻIOLANI LUAHINE
Sacred Woman of the Dance

Isn't it wonderful to have Auntie ʻIo as a
dream dancer. She's so everywhere,
in the trees, on the wind where the maile
and mokihana grows, at Polihale and
Waiʻaleʻale where the kuahu kane stands
and the punawai hoakalei that reflects
on things unknown
...ah...Auntie ʻIo Kuʻu Aloha E

Poni Kamauʻu

ʻIolani Luahine
France Haar Photographer, Honolulu, Hawaiʻi

x

A Hula Dancer always had someone watching her back.

Poni Kamauʻu

Nakʻaahiki

Esteban Artist, Kauaʻi, Hawaiʻi

MAHALO

My first teachers, Florence Grace Kini and John Ka'apuni Kini, for your love and "watching my back." Kumu Hula Hoakalei Kamau'u, Kumu Hula Kau'i Zuttermeister, and Kumu Hula Ho'oulu Cambra. Native Hawaiian scholar Rubellite Kawena Johnson and Hawaiian cultural astronomer Francis X. Warther for your integrity and generosity of spirit. My hula sisters and brothers, especially Kumu Hula Leimomi I Maldonado for your gentleness and inspiration during our performing days in Waikīkī. Mutual Publishing, especially Bennett Hymer, Jane Hopkins, and Wanni Cheung. My literary agent William Gladstone for your guidance and wisdom. Maile Meyer, Mu, Kumu Poni Kamau'u, and Kumu Sandra Kilohana Silve for your friendship, support and "seeing" the bigger message this book carries. Blair Collis and the Bishop Museum. Kay Snow-Davis for introducing Bill Gladstone, my literary agent. All the artists, poets, and writers who contributed their work. Kiyo Braverman, Saim Caglayan, Linda Ching, Cindy Conklin, Evelyn de Buhr, Al Furtado, Alaina de Havilland, Francis Haar, Francene Hart, Angela Headley, Lori Higgins, Bobby Holcomb, Arius Hopman, Isa Maria, Kathy Long, Kathy Ostman-Magnusen, Jennifer Prater, Mapuana Schneider, Dawn M. Traina, and Patricia Tsiknas for donating your artwork in support of the *Spirit of Hula* book and Halau Kaleihulumamo—Auntie 'Iolani Luahine's dream of a Resource Center and Halau that would nourish adults and children through hula and all things Hawaiian.

Martina and Mike Hough for your kōkua—Mike for your computer wizardry! My 'ohana, especially my sisters Li'ana Petranek, whose beautiful photograph inspired "Leilani" by Saim Caglayan, and Agnes Kehaulani Marti-Kini for your big generous heart. My hula 'ohana and global 'ohana—you know who you are. Beloved Kaua'i—my home and home of the Hula altars Ke Ulu o Laka and Ka Ulu o Lono—sacred temple island of initiates and teachers of teachers. And finally, my beloved son Etienne Aurelius and temple cat Puching for being my "watchers again" and "loving me 'til infinity."

xii

Forest Dancer
Kathy Long Artist, Big Island, Hawai'i

$\mathcal{I}$NTRODUCTION

"Hula is the Keeper of Codes. It holds the master key to unlocking the mind and spirit of the ancients."

Enjoyed throughout the world for its beauty, its poetry, and prayer in motion, the Hula traces its ancient roots to the beginning of time. It is sacred—a vessel and steward of a global heritage. Hula is ritual—the highest form of artistic and spiritual expression in Hawai'i. Its chants are archetypes woven by spiritual weavers of old and transmitted from master to master, Kumu Hula to Hula Kapu. Traditionally the codes and sacred rites of the Hula were kapu and taught with no alterations. The Halau Hula, school of Hula training, was dedicated to Laka and initiates performed ceremonies during auspicious celestial alignments before altars at Ka Ulu o Laka and Ka Ulu o Lono, hula heiau (temples) and platforms on Kaua'i. Ancient chants of Polynesia also incant of designated halau as "Schools of Learning" such as Malae, or Maka-Uki'u of Wailua.

Beneath the veiled codes of the chants and dance of Hula lay kaona, encoded or hidden meaning and symbols of a lineage, history, and genealogy where wisdom and eternal verities are ensconced. An alchemical dance of the cosmos, of the twin goddesses Laka and Kapo, Pele and Hi'iaka, it links us to the stellar births chanted and embraced in the kumulipo, remembered in the Pyramid Texts and expressed in some form by all indigenous cultures. A unique art, its heritage lies at the very origin of Hawaiian history and is rich in the myth, legend and lore of ancient Hawai'i and Pacifica. It chants of lōkahi, unity, the lost wisdom of the sacred feminine, cosmogony, the adepts and mystic beginnings, and the intimate embrace of lover and beloved. An active conduit between the divine and human world, the Hula is a cosmic dance played out in the heavens and in our heart, body, and soul.

As a spiritual practice, Hula awakens and engages us to our spiritual birthright as temple dancers and performers in the divine play. Hula dancers are here to prepare the temple for our children—our daughters and sons, grandchildren, and great grandchildren, the ancestors return. Each keiki o ka 'āina, child of the land, is a potential master returning to awaken our remembrances of ritual, the ancient mysteries, and sacred temples where we danced and chanted our connection to life and the stars. Their eyes radiate an innate knowing and love of the

Hawaiian culture and the Hula, and when we witness their dance, we are inspired to dance once again in the eternal matrix of mana as free spirits, priestesses and mystics, goddesses and gods, lover and beloved, watcher and keeper in rhythm with nature and the heavens.

The book you hold in your hands was conceived in celebration and meditation of the Hula. It is an invitation to walk between worlds and dance the splendor of the sacred Hula together as 'ohana, as family. With the juxtaposition of illuminating words and visuals, poetry and art, the Spirit of Hula invites you to travel the eternal realms and replicate the alchemy of mystic dancer, the union of body and soul, breath and spirit into a moment of transformation. The sacred Hula dancer, priestess, mystic, keeper, and last Hula Kapu 'Iolani Luahine spoke of this magical moment. When she danced, she said, "I am not there." She would lewa lani, transport to the highest stratum of the heavens, merge with Laka into the Spirit of Hula, the life force, essence of 'Io. Aloha no, blessings on your journey and path…and hula to your heart's delight!

Leilani Petranek

A Prayer of Adulation to Laka
He Kānaenae no Laka

In the forest, on the ridges
A ke kuahiwi, a ke kualono,

Of the mountains stands Laka;
Ku ana ʻo Laka i ke pōʻo o ka ʻohu

Dwelling in the source of the mists.
ʻO Laka kumu hula

Laka, mistress of the Hula

Nathaniel B. Emerson

1

Esteban Artist, Kaua'i, Hawai'i

Altar Prayer

Mele Kuahu

E Laka, e!

O goddess Laka!

Pupu weʻuweʻu e, Laka e!

O wildwood bouquet, O Laka!

E Laka i ka leo

O Laka, queen of the voice!

E Laka i ka loaa

O Laka, giver of gifts!

E Laka i ka waiwai

O Laka, giver of bounty!

E Laka i nā mea a pau!

O Laka, giver of all things!

Nathaniel B. Emerson

Warren Rapozo Artist, Kona, Hawai'i

Song
Oli

The rainbow stands red o'er the ocean
Kū ka pūnohu ʻula i ka moana

Mist crawls from the sea and covers the land
Hele ke ehu kai, uhi ka ʻāina

Far as Kahiki flashes the lightning
Olapa ka uila, noho i Kahiki.

A reverberant roar,
ʻUʻina, nākolo,

A shout of applause
ʻUwā ka pihe,

From the four hundred.
Lau kanaka ka hula.

I appeal to thee, Laka!
E Laka, e!

Nathaniel B. Emerson

Bobby Holcomb Artist, Huahine, French Polynesia

Dawn M. Traina Artist, Kaua'i, Hawai'i

"It is going to the altar."

'Iolani Luahine

Pele's Dream II—Hawaiian Goddesses

Linda Ching Photographer, Honolulu, Hawai'i

Hānau ke ʻāpapa nuʻu

Begotten were the gods of graded rank

Hānau ke ʻāpapa lani

Begotten were the gods of heavenly rank

Hānau Pele ka hihiʻo na lani.

Begotten was Pele, quintessence of heaven.

Nathaniel B. Emerson

Pele, Volcano Deity

Alaina de Havilland Artist, Big Island, Hawai'i

I met the Goddess Pele through a story

Papa Kini shared about Tutu and her Hula Pele.

He remembered her ecstatic dance one night

around a ceremonial fire in Waipi'o Valley.

The vision of her glistening body in sacred dance

remains in my consciousness to this

day and introduced me to the

ancient mysteries of the Hula.

Remember…

Hiʻiaka and Lohiʻau

13

Betsy Castleman-Damez Artist, Paris, France

The Goddess of the Hula let down the

celestial platform and the Kauaians built

the Hula platform,

which was the heiau of the Goddess.

The dance chant then honored the celestial

archetype which was the constellation

selected by the Goddess.

Francis X. Warther

Alaina de Havilland Artist, Big Island, Hawai'i

Kapo and Laka were one in spirit,

though their names were two.

Nathaniel Emerson

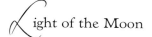

Evelyn de Buhr Artist, Kaua'i, Hawai'i

Prayer
Pule

Pele is a chiefess of Hawai'i,

'O Pele ia ali'i o Hawai'i,

chiefess of sacred darkness and of sacred light.

he ali'i no la'a uli, no la'a kea.

Mary Kawena Pukui

18

Francene Hart Artist, Big Island, Hawai'i

The sun rises, flooding the earth with light

and bringing forth life and vitality to all nature.

The Hawaiians wished for life, health, and growth

in dancing and expressed it by building the

kuahu on the east side, or side toward the sunrise.

Mary Kawena Pukui

20

Hula Kahiko Wahine—'Eono
Cindy Conklin Artist, Honolulu, Hawai'i

21

Conklin

Haumea

O Haumea, woman of Nu'umealani,

The high dwelling place of the Heavenly One.

Beautiful, dark, darkening the heavens,

Goddess of the Sacred Earth.

Goddess wife of Wākea, Sky Father.

Earth Mother from whom the bodies of

Mankind descended.

Ancestress of the Hawaiian People.

Hanaumea, sacred birth.

Mother of Pele and her Sisters.

Patroness of childbirth, Goddess of

fertility, Divine Midwife.

Entered the breadfruit tree called 'ulu.

Spirited her husband away to safety.

A breadfruit tree body, a trunk and leaves had she.

E Haumea, E Papa, E La'ila'i, E Kameha'ikana.

Many were her names.

In them all was embodied Haumea.

Dawn M. Traina

Dawn M. Traina Artist, Kaua'i, Hawai'i

Eo 'O Wai'ale'ale iluna

Wai'ale'ale, the sacred mountain that

ka nani 'o Kalani.

dwells in the beautiful heavens.

Poni Kamau'u

Esteban Artist, Kaua'i, Hawai'i

Mystical information is transmitted orally

from a master in the Hula,

thereby retaining the vital and activating

element of mana.

※

Al Furtado Artist, Honolulu, Hawai'i

The Last Dance

Alaina de Havilland Artist, Big Island, Hawai'i

Aia hoʻi!

Behold!

Mana O Hula

Hula is about giving mana.

Kathy Long Artist, Big Island, Hawai'i

Hula Motion

Sue Stagner Artist, Honolulu, Hawai'i

We go to the altar to pray for wisdom and blessings.

Poni Kamauʻu

Priestesses go forth at dawn, your hearts full of song and praise.

Kathy Burke Hula Dancer and Artist, Paris, France

The hula dancer in training was dedicated

to Laka, the hula goddess.

Hula training was a religious matter.

Total dedication was needed.

The student, man or woman,

was kapu, or set apart.

Mary Kawena Pukui

Dawn M. Traina Artist, Kaua'i, Hawai'i

I love hula for the beauty of the dance itself,

the grace of the movements and the hidden

meaning contained within the mele and ancient

chants. The messages are so beautiful.

They enrich our lives...whether one is learning

in a far off land or in the islands

—the magic is there.

Leilani Thill

Sue Stagner Artist, Honolulu, Hawaiʻi

Noʻu Koʻu Manaʻo

40

Lori Higgins Artist, Maui, Hawaiʻi

Lewa Lani!

Dance in the eternal matrix of mana.

Hula Maja Leilani O Napāli

Stephen Gnazzo Photographer, Kaua'i, Hawai'i

Na Ka Makani O Nāpali

Winds of Nāpali

Carry our message.

Into the mists we fly,

Dancing on majestic cliffs.

Our spirits soar,

Blessing parallel dimensions.

Heaven and Earth

Beloved Kaua'i

*H*awaiian Dancer

44

John Kelly, Sr. Artist, Honolulu, Hawai'i

Be Still.

Become the Dance.

Chant in the Forest

Kathy Long Artist, Big Island, Hawai'i

Spirit over Blood.

Francis X. Warther

Moon Dancer of Hawaiʻi

Alan Houghton Photographer, Honolulu, Hawaiʻi

The body is a template,

A reflection of our star origins.

When you hula

You walk between worlds.

May Day Queen

Leilani dances.

I see through tears

The shimmering white satin holokū

The pearly crown entwined with fern

White orchids and gardenia

The heavy scented strands of ivory pale wax tuberose leis.

The ipu sounds—

Kalua—Kalua—

Her body sways and sinks,

Returns and

Then sways and sinks still deeper

And those who watch at last release their breath.

Florence Grace Kini

Leilani

Saim Caglayan Artist, Kaua'i, Hawai'i amd California

Virginia Bishop Artist, Honolulu, Hawai‘i

Hula has no borders

It embraces the world

Opening hearts and minds

Bestowing Mana.

むくげのうた

Kiyo Braverman Artist, Kaua'i, Hawai'i

Now is the time to come in generosity

and share our teaching with all people.

Hula Dancers

Angela Headley Artist, Kaua'i, Hawai'i

Hula is a community of spirit

E komo mai, come join us!

The night is never long enough for dancing—

And there are not enough kisses in all the world to

Cover your beautiful smile!

Florence Grace Kini

Laka Morton Artist, Volcano, Hawai'i

Hula ʻŌlapa

60

Therese Multz Artist, Paris, France

E Hawai‘i

Sacred Land

Sanctuary of Peace

We dance in Peace

Our Hula brings Peace

Keiki's Na Kalaʻau Lesson

62

Al Furtado Artist, Honolulu, Hawaiʻi

'A'ohe pau ka 'ike i ka hālau ho'okahi.

Think not that all of wisdom resides in your halau.

Nathaniel Emerson

$\mathcal{T}$he Renewal Celebration

Bobby Holcomb Artist, Huahine, French Polynesia

Hula is simplicity of dignity and grace.

Mary Kawena Pukui

$\mathcal{L}$ovely Hula Hands

John Kelly, Sr. Artist, Honolulu, Hawai'i

Hula mai 'oe

Come to me dancing the Hula

Mary Kawena Pukui

Hula is the language of the heart

The heartbeat of the people of Hawai'i.

King David Kalākaua

Laka Morton Artist, Volcano, Hawaiʻi

Pau

Kathy Long Artist, Big Island, Hawai'i

The movement of a hand,

is a sign you make to the Most Highest.

Poni Kamauʻu

Hula Geometizes

Temple Dance, Ancient Chants

Mystic Sound, Spoken Word

Sacred Time and Sacred Space

Language of Light...

Ancient Secrets Revealed...

Hula Dancer

Svetlana Loboff Artist, Paris, France

If you believe you have something to offer,

don't hold back,

the world needs it now.

❈

Bobby Holcomb

Evelyn de Buhr Artist, Kauaʻi, Hawaiʻi

$\mathcal{W}$est Side Sunset

isa Maria Artist, Kaua'i, Hawai'i

To hula is to be the divine in motion.

In my paintings I try to convey movement and passion

and hope the viewer can hear the music as well.

My vivid colors add to the life of the dancer.

The dancer then tells the story.

A story that will live on.

Mapuana Schneider

Mapuana Baldwin Schneider Hula Dancer and Artist, Honolulu, Hawai'i

Hula gives everyone a sense of joy,

calm and being in touch with Nature.

To do a dance describing the sea or

the misty rain of a particular valley

is very grounding and uplifting for one's spirit.

The kaona hidden within the chants

speak to us across time.

Sandra Kilohana Silve

Arius Hopman Artist, Kauaʻi, Hawaiʻi

Hula ʻŌlapa

Sylef Artist, Paris, France

In Hula, We Coalese

Synergizing the traditions and codes of the Past

With the creative spirit of Ancient Future.

$\mathcal{T}$radewinds in My Hair

Kathy Ostman-Magnusen Artist, Kaua'i, Hawai'i

Adorning ourselves, we sanctify our bodies and

Embody the Hula Goddess of Light, Laka.

In perpetual ritual of sisters and brothers

We are Keepers of the sacred dance.

The Alchemy of Light and Dark

Dawn and Twilight

Body and Spirit

Sun and Moon

Merged in Lōkahi, in Sacred Union

The Goddess arises in each of us

Transforming *ALL*!

Hula in the web of color and light,

Awash in veins of sacred water.

Jennifer Prater Photographer, Kaua'i, Hawai'i

Young Girl

Your long brown hair the early

sun does brightly touch,

The goldened cheek—new breeze does quickly kiss.

I watch you go by—

Morning youth—in morning's glow

And I sigh.

Florence Grace Kini

Saim Caglayan Artist, Kaua'i, Hawai'i and California

Listen to your poet soul

It follows the kāhea of ancient voices.

Move your body, your hula hands

to the rhythmic heartbeat

of a cherished People...

Hawai'i

*H*ula Kahiko Kāne—'Ekahi
Cindy Conklin Artist, Honolulu, Hawai'i

91

Liliko'i Lady

Evelyn de Buhr Artist, Kaua'i, Hawai'i

Nui ka hānau o Limahuli i ka makani

Limahuli is fertile for those born in the wind

Kuhi ke ala ma Puʻuhinahina,

Pointing the way to Puʻuhinahina

Ua kaikoʻo lalo o Kealahula,

Rough the sea below Kealahula, going back and forth,

I ka hao a ka lawakua-o-Napali,

In the strong lawakua mountain wind of Nāpali,

Waiho wale ka luna o Puakeʻi

The top of Puakeʻi is left alone,

I honi i ke ala lauaʻe o Makana

Where you breathe the fragrance of Makana fern.

Courtesy of Rubellite Kawena Johnson

The sacred enters consciousness,

Softly through the breath of chant—

Mele Hula

Wherein lay the codes of initiation,

Ever evolving...

Evoking the dancer's transformation,

In deep resonance with Global Transformation.

95

Esteban Artist, Kaua'i, Hawai'i

In Hula we are dancing the "Game of Life"

on an archetype of the Cosmos,

built to activate the Cosmos.

It is the origin of how you dance

and why you dance.

Francis X. Warther

𝓗ula Kahiko Wahine—'Ekolu
Cindy Conklin Artist, Honolulu, Hawai'i

97

Kāhea

Jennifer Prater Photographer, Kauaʻi, Hawaiʻi

Hula is a world we must respectfully enter—

Where dance, spirit and nature's love are united,

and where dance is so deeply connected to the daily life.

Elizabeth Zana

Hōpoe

Kathy Burke Hula Dancer and Artist, Paris, France

Some of these dances have been danced by generations

and generations of Hawaiian dancers.

I like to think that in turn we add our own

spirit to that, and so it passes on...

Stephanie Rigg

102

Mapuana Baldwin Schneider Hula Dancer and Artist, Honolulu, Hawaiʻi

Let the spirit of hula dance in and out of your heart.

Open the window of Aloha

Heal the World.

Hula Noho with Pūʻili

Theresa Multz Hula Dancer and Artist, Paris, France

GLOSSARY

'Ekahi	One
'Ekolu	Three
'Eono	Six
Halau	Hula school, Hula troupe or corps
Hina	Most widely known goddess in Polynesia, Moon Goddess
Holokū	Dress with a train
Ho'omākaukau	A Hula command, prepares the dancers to begin dance
Ho'olewa	To float
Hula	To dance; the national dance of Hawai'i
Hula 'auana	Modern Hula
Hula kahiko	Traditional Hula
Hula olapa	Hula dancer
Hula kala'au	Hula using a dancing stick
'Io	Hawaiian hawk, essence
Ipu Heke	Double gourd, musical instrument
Kāhea	To call, to name; recital of the first lines of a stanza as a cue to chanter
Keiki	Child
Kuahu	Altar
Kumu Hula	Dance master, literal meaning—the source
Laka	Goddess and patron of the Hula
Mana	Supernatural or divine power, spiritual
Mele Hula	Chant accompanying a hula, poetry accompanied by dance movement
Oli	Chant, chanted poetry not intended for dancing
Pau	Finish, the end, complete
Pele	Volcano goddess, subject of Mele Hula
Pule	Prayer

105

ARTIST CREDITS

Virginia Bishop
I Love Hawai'i

artseries@aol.com

Betsy Castleman-Damez
Hi'iaka and Lohi'au

betsydamez@yahoo.fr

Kiyo Braverman
Song of Hibiscus

P.O. Box 729
Anahola, HI 96703

Linda Ching
Pele's Dream II
Hawaiian Goddesses

www.lindaching.com

Kathy Burke
Ho'omākaukau

Kathyburke@parisportraits.com

Cindy Conklin
Hula Kahiko Kāne—'Ekahi

home1.gte.net/conklin

Kathy Burke
Hōpoe

Kathyburke@parisportraits.com

Cindy Conklin
Hula Kahiko Wahine—'Ekolu

home1.gte.net/conklin

Saim Caglayan
Hula by the Bay

www.jskn.com/saim.html

Cindy Conklin
Hula Kahiko Wahine—'Eono

home1.gte.net/conklin

Saim Caglayan
Leilani

www.jskn.com/saim.html

C. H. Davis
Beautiful Wahine

www.chdavis.com

Evelyn de Buhr
Light of the Moon

4920 Wailapa
Kīlauea, HI 96754

Evelyn de Buhr
Liliko'i Lady

4920 Wailapa
Kīlauea, HI 96754

Evelyn de Buhr
Sister Love

4920 Wailapa
Kīlauea, HI 96754

Alaina de Havilland
Hina

alainadeh@hawaii.rr.com

Alaina de Havilland
The Last Dance

alainadeh@hawaii.rr.com

Alaina de Havilland
Pele, Volcano Deity

alainadeh@hawaii.rr.com

Esteban (Steve Davis)
Hanakāpī'ai Dancer

www.stevedavisartist.com

Esteban (Steve Davis)
Ho'olewa

www.stevedavisartist.com

Esteban (Steve Davis)
Naka'ahiki

www.stevedavisartist.com

Esteban (Steve Davis)
Pōhaku

www.stevedavisartist.com

Al Furtado
The Chanter

www.merchanthawaii.com

Al Furtado
Keiki's Na Kala'au Lesson

www.merchanthawaii.com

Stephen Gnazzo
Hula Maja Leilani o Nāpali

www.youreventimages.com

Francis Haar
'Iolani Luahine

tomhaar@lava.net

Francene Hart
Compassionate Pele

www.francenehart.com

Angela Headley
Hula Dancers

slandart.sail@verizon.net

Lori Higgins
No'u Ko'u Mana'o

www.lorihiggins.com

Bobby Holcomb
The 'Aparima Dance in Honor of Laka, Goddess of Dance

Dorotea7@mail.pf

Bobby Holcomb
The Renewal Celebration

Dorotea7@mail.pf

Arius Hopman
Tahiti Fête—Rohotu Halau

www.hopmanart.com

Alan Houghton
Moon Dancer of Hawai'i

www.art-broker.com

isa Maria
West Side Sunset

www.isamaria.com

John Kelly, Sr.
Hawaiian Dancer

4117 Blackpoint Road
Honolulu, HI 96816

John Kelly, Sr.
Lovely Hula Hands

4117 Blackpoint Road
Honolulu, HI 96816

Florence Grace Kini
Hula Dancer Leilani

inspirit11@hotmail.com

Svetlana Loboff
Hula Dancer

koutiou@freesurf.fr

Kathy Long
Chant in the Forest

bklong@wwwdb.org

Kathy Long
Forest Dancer

bklong@wwwdb.org

Kathy Long
Mana

bklong@wwwdb.org

Kathy Long
Pau

bklong@wwwdb.org

Laka Morton
Happy Talk

P.O. Box 1121
Volcano, HI 96785

Laka Morton
Limahuli

P.O. Box 1121
Volcano, HI 96785

Therese Multz
Hula Noho with Pūʻili

tmultz@aol.com

Therese Multz
Hula ʻŌlapa

tmultz@aol.com

Kathy Ostman-Magnusen
Tradewinds in My Hair

www.kathysart.com

Jennifer Prater
Kāhea

www.islandechoesphotography.com

Jennifer Prater
Pule

www.islandechoesphotography.com

Mapuana Baldwin Schneider
Hula ʻAuana

www.mapuanagallery.com

Warren Rapozo
Essence of Hula

www.rapozo-studio.com

Mapuana Baldwin Schneider
Swing

www.mapuanagallery.com

Warren Rapozo
Silent Preparation

www.rapozo-studio.com

Sue Stagner
Hula Motion

2708 A Oʻahu Avenue
Honolulu, HI 96822

Sue Stagner
Kahiko

2708 A O'ahu Avenue
Honolulu, HI 96822

Sylef (Sylvain Lef)
Aia Lā o Pele

sylvainlef@club-internet.fr

Sylef (Sylvain Lef)
Hula Olapa

sylvainlef@club-internet.fr

Dawn M. Traina
Haumea

Box 654/3840 Hanapēpē Road
Hanapēpē, HI 96716

Dawn M. Traina
Hula Kāla'au

Box 654/3840 Hanapepe Road
Hanapepe, HI 96716

Dawn M. Traina
Ipu Heke

Box 654/3840 Hanapēpē Road
Hanapēpē, HI 96716

Patricia Tsiknas
'Io

patricia@gardenofthereal.com

BIBLIOGRAPHY

Barrere, Dorothy, Mary Kawena Pukui, Marion Kelly. *Hula, Historical Perspectives*. Bishop Museum. Honolulu: 1980.

Emerson, Nathaniel. *Unwritten Literature of Hawaii: The Sacred Songs of the Hula*. Government Printing Office. Washington DC: 1909.

ABOUT THE AUTHOR

Leilani Petranek was raised under the majestic Koʻolau mountains in the little town of Kaʻaʻawa on Oʻahu by Florence Grace Kini, an Austrian-Hungarian German poet and John Kaʻapuni Kini, a pure blooded Native Hawaiian fisherman from Waipiʻo Valley on the Big Island of Hawaiʻi. She received her first Hula lessons at the age of nine from Kumu Hula Kauʻi Zuttermeister. While completing her Hawaiian Studies degree at the University of Hawaiʻi at Mānoa, she continued her Hula training with Kumu Hula Hoakalei Kamauʻu and Oli training, traditional chants, with Hoʻoulu Cambra.

An accomplished Hula dancer and choreographer, Leilani appeared on national and international television and in movies, and performed on stage at the Hilton Hawaiian Village's Tapa Room, Danny Kaleikini Show, Tavana's Tahitian Revue, Radio City Music Hall, Ceasar's Palace Las Vegas, Nagoya Castle Hotel Japan and other venues.

A sacred dancer of numerous traditions, she now works as a writer, producer, broadcaster, and cultural liaison. Leilani is the Hawaiʻi producer/interviewer for the award-winning Smithsonian "Living Voices" radio series featuring Native American and Native Hawaiian profiles, and is the producer of the "Spirit of Learning Film." She lives on the island of Kauaʻi with her beloved son Etienne and temple cat Puching. *Spirit of Hula: Mana O Hula* is her first book.

Hula O Leilani

Private Collection of Leilani Petranek